Home Business Success Strategies

10 Home-Based Businesses You Can Start Quickly and Inexpensively

James Adam

Copyright © 2018 by James Adam

All rights reserved. The contents of this book may not be reproduced, duplicated or transmitted without direct written permission from the author.

Under no circumstances will any legal responsibility or blame be held against the publisher for any reparation, damages, or monetary loss due to the information herein, either directly or indirectly.

Legal Notice:

This book is copyright protected. This is only for personal use. You cannot amend, distribute, sell, use, quote or paraphrase any part or the content within this book without the consent of the author.

Disclaimer Notice:

Please note the information contained within this document is for educational and entertainment purposes only. Every attempt has been made to provide accurate, up to date and complete, reliable information. No warranties of any kind are expressed or implied. Readers acknowledge that the author is not engaging in the rendering of legal, financial, medical or professional advice. The content of this book has been derived from various sources. Please consult a licensed professional before attempting any techniques outlined in this book.

By reading this document, the reader agrees that under no circumstances is the author responsible for any losses, direct or indirect, which are incurred as a result of the use of information contained within this document, including, but not limited to, —errors, omissions, or inaccuracies.

Contents

Introduction 1

Chapter 1 - Blog Page 2

Chapter 2 - YouTube Channel 7

Chapter 3 - Amazon FBA 11

Chapter 4 - Affiliate Marketing 18

Chapter 5 - Video Services 22

Chapter 6 - Freelance Writing Services 25

Chapter 7 - Self-Publishing 27

Chapter 8 - Private Label Rights Products (PLR) ... 29

Chapter 9 - Social Media Management 32

Chapter 10 - Virtual Assistant 34

Conclusion 38

INTRODUCTION

It's very challenging to work as an employee these days. More than just the lack of personal freedom, it often entails braving the morning and evening rush hour traffic and is often boring. No wonder many people want to be their own bosses, including you!

In this book, you'll learn 10 different home-based businesses you can start and gradually build to eventually become a fully-fledged run-from-home business that can allow you to quit your boring job and experience the financial and personal freedom that many others have already experienced. With these 10 home-based businesses, it's possible to have your cake and eat it too. And if it's the kind of life you want, turn the page and let's begin!

CHAPTER 1 - BLOG PAGE

While blogging isn't a get-rich-quick business that you can do at home (or just about), it is very possible to make good money out of it and blog for a living. You'll definitely need good writing skills, perseverance and discipline but hey, what business or financial endeavor doesn't require perseverance and discipline to succeed in?

If you're wondering how in the world is it possible to create and maintain a blog and earn a good living from it from the comfort of your own home or just about anywhere else you'd like to work, then wonder no more. And the best part of it - as well as with the 9 other home-based businesses you can start now - is that you can even start it for free or at most, for very little initial capital. You can immediately register for a free blog site from platforms like wordpress.com or via self-hosted platforms like WordPress.org. And the primary way you can make money off it is through advertisements.

CPM or CPC Ads

CPM ads - or Cost per Thousand Impression ads - are those where advertisers on your website will pay you a specific sum of money based on the number of people who see or view your ads, which are in multiples of 1,000s. CPC - or Cost per Click ads - on the other hand are those that pay you a fixed amount of money every time someone clicks on a banner ad that an advertising network places on your blog site, such as Google AdSense. Usually, CPC ads appear as banner ads on websites.

CPM or CPC ads are placed on your websites indirectly via advertising networks, first and foremost of which is Google AdSense. The way it works is that Google AdSense will determine which ads will appear on your blog site based on its content. This way, you don't have to scour the

Internet for advertisers on your blog site. By enrolling under the Google AdSense program, all you'll need to worry about is generating good content and attracting subscribers or regular visitors to your site. The advertising part is Google's job.

If, for some reason, you abhor Google, don't fret. There are other advertising networks that you can use such as Media.net, Infolinks, and Chitika. Yes, Google doesn't have a monopoly, though it corners practically the entire online advertising network these days.

Private Ads

While working with advertising networks can make it much easier for you to populate your website with advertisers, there's a tradeoff: smaller advertising revenue. Because these networks practically carry the burden of looking for advertisements to place on your website, they deserve the biggest chunk of advertising fees paid by advertisers. So if you want to earn more from your blog site's ads, you'll have to look for advertisers yourself so that you'll get the entire advertising revenue. This type of ad is called private ad because you're responsible for looking for advertisers on your blog site.

While CPC or CPM ads mostly come in the form of banners, private ads can be in the form of links, buttons, or banners - whatever floats your boat! This is because they're dealing with you directly and being in complete control over your blog site, you can give advertisers options as to how their ads will appear on your blog site.

Sponsored Posts

Sponsored posts are better than private or public ads in the sense that you can charge more money for it. Why? It's because of the form in which it appears. With sponsored posts, you'll create a blog post that's exclusively about the advertiser's product or service. It's not just going to be an advertisement, but in a way, it's an endorsement on your end. Or you can write a blog post that's directly related to the advertiser's product or service and then mention at any point in the post that the post was "Brought to you by _____."

With sponsored posts, there are different arrangements you can make with advertisers. It can be a one-time payment, a recurring payment, or a one-time payment based on the number of people who've read the post within a specific period of time, among others. It's really between you and your advertisers, but the bottom line is you have enough flexibility in terms of payment arrangements when it comes to sponsored posts.

CHAPTER 2 - YOUTUBE CHANNEL

Have you ever wondered how your favorite YouTubers are able to find so much time for creating videos on a regular basis as if they didn't have to work to earn a living and support their YouTube channels? Well, wonder no more because in this chapter, you'll learn how you can make a living from YouTube channels from the comfort of your own home.

Advertisements

Just like a blog site, you can also earn advertising income from your YouTube Channel videos. The keys to successfully doing this are high-quality and engaging videos and enough viewership. Let me explain.

Home Business Success Strategies

As of January 2018, YouTube channels can qualify for advertising - i.e., monetizing videos via ads - once they are able to accumulate a minimum of 4,000 watching hours in the last 12 months and a minimum of 1,000 subscribers. So in your case, you'll need to have at least 1,000 people subscribe to your channel and accumulate a minimum of 4,000 viewing hours for it within a 12-month period, which is the viewership requirement.

Where do high quality videos come in? Simple - you won't be able to achieve the required viewership requirements if your YouTube channel has crappy video content. It's that simple. You need high quality videos to make enough people watch enough hours of your video to qualify for advertising income.

The primary model for YouTube advertising is the CPC or cost per click model. And to qualify for YouTube's advertising or monetization program, here are the following steps:

James Adam

1. Read and agree with YouTube's terms and conditions by enabling your channel's monetization feature. To do this, click on your account's icon at the upper right hand of the screen, click on Creator Studio, choose Channel, then Status, and finally features. From there, you'll see the Enable option under Monetization - click on it. Then just follow the on-screen instructions for accepting the YouTube Partner Program's conditions and terms.

2. Sign up for a Google AdSense account, which is fairly easy and is free.

3. Choose the types of ads you prefer to be shown on your channel's videos and enable automatic monetization for all your channel's existing and coming videos. When your application for the Partner Program gets approved, your videos will start earning advertising income. Click on save.

4. Wait for YouTube to finish reviewing your application.

Direct Product Placements/Sponsorships

Similar to the sponsored posts advertising income option for blog sites, you can also earn from direct sponsorships or product placements on your channel. Under this scenario, you can charge advertisers money for featuring their products and services in your videos via mentions, endorsements, or product reviews.

Content Is King

Remember, if there's one thing you must focus your resources and time on when it comes to making a living via your YouTube channel, it's this: Content is King! If you don't post high-quality videos, might as well kiss your dreams of making a living via YouTube from the comfort of your home goodbye. Remember, focus on content and the rest will follow.

CHAPTER 3 - AMAZON FBA

FBA stands for Fulfillment by Amazon.com, which is a program that allows you to have your own online store on the Amazon.com platform. And more than just having a place to sell your goods online, the FBA program takes care of your online store's fulfillment needs, i.e., inventory management, logistics management, and records management. All you need to focus on are promoting your products and making sure you always have enough inventory on your Amazon FBA store.

You may be wondering, why should you sign up with Amazon FBA if you can have your own online store instead and keep all of the revenues? Well, let me count the reasons why:

- Logistics: Not only can you afford not to worry about the cost of delivering physical products to your buyers, but you can also deliver them faster. Can you imagine the huge amount of additional work you'll need to do to just to ship your products to your buyers yourself? And it's not just shipping. Amazon FBA also takes care of product returns for you.

- Exposure: Because Amazon is the world's biggest online store, it goes without saying that it attracts a lot of serious buyers. And where most of the serious buyers converge, the market is for your products is huge. If you just sell your products on an online store you put up and maintain yourself, you'll have to do a lot to draw in even just a fraction of Amazon's buyer traffic.

- Credibility: Being on the Amazon platform requires being able to establish your business' legitimacy. Just by being on the

Amazon platform is enough validation that you're not a fly-by-night online store, which can go a long way in making a lot of online buyers trust you enough to buy from you.

- Payment Security: Being under the Amazon FBA program means you can use Amazon's highly secure payment system, which is a big plus because it can help make buyers feel more secure about buying from your FBA store as compared to your own online store only.

Product Is King

If content is king when it comes to blog sites and YouTube channels, it's the product itself that is king in Amazon FBA. In particular, choosing the right product can significantly increase your chances of being able to successfully create a home-based business that you can run even by yourself.

So what makes a product the "right" one? Among the considerations are:

- Competition: The less competition, the better. Why? It's because more competition makes it harder to price your products well for your benefit because competition drives prices down. Possible indicators of serious competition in your product or market include competitors ranked in the Top 5,000 bestseller ranks in your product's category or well-known brand names in the same category or niche.

- Price: The ideal price range for products sold in the FBA program lie between $10 and $50.

- Weight: The lighter your products are, the lower their shipping costs will be, which means it's more sellable and profitable.

- Durability: Products that can easily break will drive up your costs and eat at your business' profitability. So go for tough products as much as possible.

- Profit Margin: Only products that you can sell for a minimum profit margin of 75% will make it worth your business while. Anything lower? Think about them seriously.

Keys to Success

If you want to optimize your chances of successfully, then you'll have to be very cognizant of the following factors, which accounted for the success of so many Amazon FBA sellers:

- Economies of Scale: Generally speaking, selling more units of a good is a lot more cost efficient compared to selling less units. But as with many small business owners, logistics is a major concern for increasing the number of units sold. Because Amazon FBA takes care of the logistics side of your business, achieving economies of scale is much easier, making your business more cost efficient and ultimately, more profitable.

- Objectivity: You will encounter moments when you'll make errors in judgment and when you do make them, it's important to see them for what they are, learn from them, and make the necessary adjustments. If you're the type who's emotional and unable to easily adjust to changes in situations, it'll be hard for you to succeed with Amazon FBA.

- Time Frame: All businesses take time to become profitable and sustainable. As such, you must get into this with a medium to long-term perspective. Not weeks, not months, but at least 1 to 2 years. Otherwise, you'll probably quit before your Amazon FBA business starts churning in profit.

- Focus: The most successful Amazon FBA business owners are those that stick to just one niche and their various products are all involved in that one niche. They don't sell many products that aren't related to each other and from different niches.

- Discipline: As with any business, whether home-based or not, you will need to keep a tight rein on your budget, spending, and perseverance, which is highly needed in the first few months of your FBA business. If you do whatever you feel and don't do what's needed because it doesn't feel good or because you find it too cumbersome, your chances of successfully running a profitable home-based business with FBA is low.

CHAPTER 4 - AFFILIATE MARKETING

Selling products online can post some major challenges as a home-based entrepreneur, especially if you're under budget and can't afford to stock up enough inventory because of cost. If you don't have a big enough capital to work with, you may not be able to store enough inventory to generate big enough sales to establish a profitable home-based online store business, even if it's through FBA, which only provides logistical support and not a financial one. And even FBA entails payment of certain fees to avail of their program.

Another challenge with selling online - even if you have the capital - is inventory. And when it comes to inventory, we're not just talking about having enough of it. We're also talking about having the right kind of inventory, which can spell the difference between having your money stuck in slow-moving (if at all) inventory.

If you feel that such challenges are insurmountable for you with regards to creating a home-based, online selling business, fret not! A very good alternative is affiliate marketing. But what is it?

Affiliate marketing is a business where you help online vendors of mostly digital products sell their stuff online. You help them do so by referring prospects to them and when those prospects buy the vendors' products, you get paid commission income. Take note that you don't even have to sell the stuff under affiliate marketing. All you'll need to do is drive traffic to the vendors' sales websites and from there, it's their responsibility to convince the prospects you referred to them to buy.

So what's your guarantee that the vendor will be able to clearly identify which of their prospects who buy their products came from your referral so that they can properly pay you your commissions? When you get approved to promote their products, you will be given a unique affiliate link, which you'll embed in all your online promotional content that your viewers can click to be directed to vendors' sales pages. Through affiliate links, online vendors will be able to properly tag sales that resulted from your referrals and pay you the commissions due to you.

How It Works

Sign up for a free affiliate account on either or both of the world's two biggest affiliate marketing platforms, which are JVZoo and Clickbank. Just go to JVZoo.com or Clickbank.com and follow their instructions on how to sign up for an affiliate account on their platform.

Once your account's set up, you can scout for the best-selling products on those platforms that belong to the niche you want to focus on and ask their respective vendors to allow you to promote their products. If after evaluation the vendors approve your application, you'll be given your unique affiliate link that you will embed in all your online promotional content to drive prospects to the vendors' sales pages. If they buy, you get paid commissions. It's that simple.

With affiliate marketing, you don't need to come up with your own products or stock your own inventory. You'll simply be riding on established business systems for selling mostly digital products. All you'll need to do is promote such products online!

CHAPTER 5 - VIDEO SERVICES

If you're like me who is an avid video-creating hobbyist and you're really good at it, why not consider making a living out of it from your own home? And I'm not just talking about creating your own YouTube channel and monetizing it. I'm talking about helping others with their own video-creation or editing needs via your own online video services business.

So how do you do it? You can sign up for an account with 3 of the world's biggest job outsourcing platforms: UpWork (formerly known as oDesk), Freelancer, or Fiverr. And once your account's up and running, upload samples of your awesome portfolio on your profile pages for each of those accounts so you can wow prospective clients right off the bat. Populate your blog site (if you have one), YouTube channel (a big advantage if you have one, even if you don't monetize it), and social media profile pages with your created videos too and provide links to them on your profile pages so that when you bid for video projects on said platforms, you'll have something awesome to show prospects that will convince them that you're worth hiring for their video creation needs.

A minimal investment in royalty-free stock video clips, soundtracks, and images is crucial here. It's because you can get in trouble - as well as your clients - if you use copyrighted video clips, soundtracks, or images on your projects, which can ruin both your and your clients' reputations. And if you're a serious video-creation hobbyist, you'd know the importance of having access to soundtracks, video clips, and images, right? Right.

Two other important investments - albeit relatively small ones - you'll need to make for providing excellent video creation services that don't cost an arm and a leg are Animatron and Viddyoze. Animatron is an online video animation platform that you can use to create awesome animation videos, which are perfect for explainer and advertising videos. Viddyoze is a platform where you can easily create professional-quality and stunning video clips that are essential for online branding and marketing such as logo intros, transition and outro clips. From experience, having both is a very great way to leapfrog over many other video service providers in the market today as a beginner.

CHAPTER 6 - FREELANCE WRITING SERVICES

As with video services, you can also establish a home-based freelance writing business via the 3 major platforms mentioned earlier: UpWork, Freelancer, and Fiverr. Because of the current boom in online marketing, which is expected to stay for the long-term, demand for freelance writing services is high and will continue to remain high. So if you're very good with writing, especially copywriting and non-fiction content writing, you can sign up for a free account with either or all of the 3 above-mentioned platforms and start bidding for gigs that can eventually become a regular business.

Later on when you've established yourself as an in-demand writer, you can put up your own online freelance or ghostwriting agency by hiring a pool of freelance writers and farming out the projects you get to them at a much lower rate so you can still earn good income. Through an online freelance writing agency, you can easily scale up the number of writing projects you can take on and ultimately, your income, and work even less.

CHAPTER 7 - SELF-PUBLISHING

With the advent of the Internet and platforms such as the Amazon.com Kindle Store, self-publishing and marketing books has never been so easy! Unlike in generations past, you will no longer need to go through a big publishing company just to put out your own book and earn a lot of moolah from it. Using your computer, some simple software like Word/Pages and PowerPoint/Keynote/Pixlr, you can write, package, and publish your own e-books all by yourself with little or no cost at all, and keep most of the revenues generated from sales of such. Just sign up for an account with Amazon.com's Kindle Direct Publishing (KDP) program and follow their guidelines and instructions for uploading and selling your own e-book on their platform. By the way, the Kindle Store is the world's biggest library so by self-publishing on that platform alone, you have access to millions and millions of potential readers and buyers.

But what if you're not a writer or a graphic artist who can create your own covers? No problem! You can hire ghostwriters and/or graphic artists on the 3 major platforms mentioned earlier: UpWork, Freelancer, and Fiverr or even use the Writer's Summit. Just tell them the book you want to have written, the outline or topics to cover, word count, and design. Then you can upload their finished product, which is branded under your own name as author, on the Kindle Store and you can have your very first self-published book.

CHAPTER 8 - PRIVATE LABEL RIGHTS PRODUCTS (PLR)

Selling digital products - like self-published e-books or video courses - is one of the best and cheapest home-based businesses you can establish. But a specific challenge that most digital marketing wannabes face when it comes to creating such a business is content generation. If you don't have the skills or knowledge to create your own e-books or courses, you can outsource them. But if you're under a very strict and low budget, you may not be able to afford hiring freelancers to do it for you. And if you're perfectly capable of creating your own digital content, you'll still face the challenge of having to spend a lot of time creating digital content, which can be very challenging if you have a day job that takes up a lot of your time and other responsibilities.

Home Business Success Strategies

Regardless if you're able to create your own content or not, you will also need to create good online marketing resources to promote your digital products such as emails, sales pages, or sales videos, which could add more cost, time, or both. And this is where PLR or private label rights products come into play.

PLRs are digital products that you can buy, which include the right to resell them as they are or as rebranded or revised products while keeping all profits to yourself. And the best part of it all is that most good quality PLRs are cheap. The most expensive one I got cost me a total of $50.00 only, which I was able to recover after only 2 sales!

You can sell PLRs on a stand-alone basis or as part of a bigger package with other PLRs or your own digital product. You can also use them to help promote your own digital products more effectively by packaging them as bonuses for buying such. You can get quality PLRs from websites like IDPLR,

James Adam

Master Resale Rights, JVZoo, WarriorPlus, and Unstoppable PLR.

CHAPTER 9 - SOCIAL MEDIA MANAGEMENT

Believe it or not, you can create a legit, home-based business from something you're already doing intuitively and with a lot of fun - social media. In particular, I'm talking about managing other people's or business' social media accounts!

If you're wondering if there's an actual demand for it, think about your favorite celebrities who are very, very busy. Do you think they have the time to always be on their official social media pages to post regular quality content and engage their fans on an almost real-time basis? Probably not. And if that's the case, how do you think they're able to manage their official social media accounts well? You guessed it - social media managers.

It's the same with businesses. Big businesses assign people to do nothing all day (and probably all night too) but manage social media accounts. And if you're a small business owner who's doing practically all things related to managing your business, you probably won't have enough time and energy to manage your business' social media account well enough for effective marketing.

Now, can you see why there's an actual demand for social media management services?

As with freelance writing and video services gigs, you can start by going to platforms such as UpWork and Freelancer to book your first gigs. Give it your best shot and over time, it can become a very good home-based business for you.

CHAPTER 10 - VIRTUAL ASSISTANT

A virtual assistant is a person who provides another person or a business with support services via the Internet from another location. Support services include a wide range of services from social media promotion to general administrative functions (e.g., appointment setting, bookkeeping, email management, etc.). Practically anybody who needs to get a lot of things done for their businesses or professional careers benefit from hiring virtual assistants, which can include professional bloggers, sole proprietors, service professionals, and small entrepreneurs who simply don't have the time or skills to handle repetitive, low value but necessary tasks related to their businesses. By hiring virtual assistants, VAs for brevity, they can free up most of their time so they can focus on things that provide more value for their businesses such as marketing, prospecting, and developing new businesses.

Aside from work experience, you'll need to be honest, patient, personable, organized, professional, and exercise discretion as a VA.

Pick the Right Niche

One of the worst things you can do to start a VA home-based business or career is to aimlessly or thoughtlessly get gigs in various niches that you don't have much working experience on. Why? If you choose to work as a VA in a line of business whose support services requirements aren't within your expertise or experience, you may end up performing poorly and ruin your chances of getting higher paying gigs moving forward when you get very low ratings and negative feedback on outsourcing sites like UpWork and Freelancer. While there's no hard and fast rules for what makes for the "right" niche, one of the best indicators of such is that the required work is well within your skills and working experience. Another is if it's something you're very passionate and knowledgeable about.

A Virtual Assistance Agency

If you want to eventually scale your business up, you will need to "transform" into an agency. Why? Because your ability to earn income as a VA yourself is tied to the amount of time you can put into your work and given all of us have limited time daily (max of 24 hours in case you're wondering, which we really can't optimize for work as we all need to rest, eat, and do other things), the income you can earn from being a VA is limited, even if it can be really good.

As an agency, you hire other VAs under you, get more gigs than what you can personally work on, and farm them out to your hired VAs. You can get as many gigs as you want by hiring as many VAs needed under your agency, which means you can scale up your VA income as much as you want - all from the comforts of your own home!

CONCLUSION

Thank you for buying this book. I hope that through it, you were able to learn some of the best ways to start your own home-based business or businesses quickly and cheaply. But more importantly, I hope that through this book, you were encouraged to take action, regardless of how small it is, to start working on putting up your own home-based business. The best action to take from this point forward is to learn more about setting up such businesses so you can hit the ground running as soon as possible. Remember, knowledge is just potential power. It becomes actual power the moment it's applied. So go ahead, act now.

Here's to your home-bases entrepreneurial success my friend! Cheers!

References: None as I'm familiar with the topic.

www.ingramcontent.com/pod-product-compliance
Lightning Source LLC
Chambersburg PA
CBHW031504210526
45463CB00003B/1068